CW00420250

The
feckin' book of
Irish Sex & Love
that's not fit
for dacent
people's eyes

Colin Murphy & Donal O'Dea

THE O'BRIEN PRESS
DUBLIN

First published 2005 by The O'Brien Press Ltd,
20 Victoria Road, Dublin 6, Ireland.
Tel: +353 1 4923333; Fax: +353 1 4922777
E-mail: books@obrien.ie
Website: www.obrien.ie

ISBN: 0-86278-921-4

British Library Cataloguing-in-Publication Data
A catalogue reference for this book is available from the British Library.

1 2 3 4 5 6 7 8 9 10
05 06 07 08 09

Printed in Hungary

WARNING!

This book contains the word 'sex' 44 times. Sorry, make that 45 times.

Abstinence from sex: This will make you a better person. At least that's what the Church has been trying to beat into us since ancient times. The bishops really got stuck into the 'no sex please, we're Irish' thing around the seventh century, beginning with their own priests, most of whom were married, and in

LET ME GET THIS STRAIGHT... YOU ABSTAIN FROM SEX FOR THE WHOLE YEAR EXCEPT FOR ONE SINGLE NIGHT... WHAT MAKES YOU SO HAPPY?

IT'S TONIGHT! IT'S TONIGHT!

one decree banned sex on so many occasions (Lent, Advent, Sundays, the day the bin-man came, etc) that opportunities for a quick grope were limited to five minutes on a Tuesday after-noon in August.

Adultery: Adultery is, of course, a sin. And in the eyes of the Irish Catholic church, looking at one's wife lustfully is also a form of adultery. So, if you want to make love to your wife after you've had the Chinese takeaway and bottle of

SORRY LOVE, IT'S THE NEW DRESS DESIGNED BY THE CHURCH TO STOP US COMMITTING ADULTERY

red, you should go around blindfold for several hours beforehand. This may make trimming the hedge or fixing the kitchen shelf a little tricky, but at least you can enjoy your semi-drunken tumble without a mark on your soul, although your body may look like it's been through a meat grinder.

Agony Aunts: Typical question to an Irish agony aunt in the 1960s–1980s: 'If a boy squeezes my breast will I become pregnant?' Typical answer: 'No, but breast-squeezing is a sin anyway, whether you're the squeezer or the squeezee. Go to confession and don't do it again.' Among the foremost dispensers of coy advice on our love lives were Angela McNamara and Frankie Byrne. When the phenomenon of the ultra conservative agony aunt disappeared, it solved a lot of problems.

Archbishop John Charles McQuaid: From 1940 to 1972, the Archbishop directed the course of the nation in issues of morality, and for his purposes this meant everything. It included forbidding the importation of tampons as they might make women excited! Considering Dev actually got this guy to approve the 1937 Constitution before showing it to the cabinet, it's probably not surprising how sexually screwed up we were as a nation for the next half century or so. (For issues upon which he had a direct influence see also Abstinence, Adultery, Celibacy, Censorship, Contrac... ah, what the hell, see the whole damn book!)

Bachelor Festivals: The Ballybunion and Mullingar Bachelor Festivals offer the opportunity for eligible bachelors to make eejits of themselves in front of hordes of women, who get to holler obscenities just like men. The winner, one assumes, can expect to be ineligible for next year's competition. In the

1970s the Ballybunion one was misleadingly called The Gay Bachelor Festival – gay in those days implying jolly and carefree. The 'Gay' bit was dropped, presumably after a few of the candidates displayed a distinct lack of interest in girls.

Bishop Eamonn Casey: After centuries of sexual repression, the dam finally burst in 1992. And we owe it all to Eamo. Never shy to denounce the evils of pre-marital sex, it turned out that the bould bishop had had a booboo or two of his own in this regard, literally. Luckily, he was caught by the short and curlies, and the rejection of the Church's teachings on sex has been snowballing ever since. For this we owe Bishop Casey a large debt of gratitude and he deserves a huge erection (of a statue) in his honour.

ERECTED
IN HONOUR
OF BISHOP
EAMONN CASEY

Book Bans: Between the 1920s and the 1950s the number of books banned in Ireland rose from a handful to thousands. To shrieks of 'Eureka! I found a dirty word' the works of the likes of H G Wells, Orwell, Hemingway, Chandler remained off limits to Irish eyes. During this sad chapter, countless books by Irish writers – James Joyce, Frank O'Connor, Edna O'Brien, etc – also had an unhappy ending. In a three-month period in 1952, one member of the Censorship Board, C J O'Reilly, examined seventy books. He also banned seventy books! Ah, God be with the good oul' days.

Brehon Laws: The Brehon Laws are now recognised as the most advanced legal system in the ancient world. Under Brehon law, for example, women were equal partners in a marriage, of which there were ten forms. These included a marriage called the 7th degree union, which is extremely popular nowadays. It's called a one-night stand.

Celibacy: If we've learnt one thing about celibate priests in Ireland, it's that priests in Ireland largely aren't. And, in reality, there is no basis for them to be celibate in the first place. St Peter was married and some Popes were actually the daddies of other Popes. Similarly, in ancient Ireland farmer traditionally begat farmer, judge begat judge and priest begat priest. Until Pope Gregory VII came and screwed it up for everyone in 1079. After that, misery begat misery.

Censorship: Censorship in Ireland had reached such extremes in the 1930s-1950s that the Church/State used to employ an army of folk to cut ads for lingerie out of foreign magazines coming into the country. During this sad era, thousands of books, films, and even poems were banned or censored for containing the most innocuous references to sex or for using 'swear words'. So, to the bullies who would gladly return us to those dark days, we'd like to say the following: Arse. Boobs. Orgasm.

Charles Stewart Parnell/
Kitty O'Shea: Either the most famous or
infamous love story in Irish history, depending on your point of view. Parnell, MP and Irish Nationalist leader, had a fling with Kitty O'Shea, the missus of a close party aide, William O'Shea. Surprisingly, Willie wasn't too put out, but when he decided to cut Kitty loose, the entire affair came out in the divorce proceedings. Parnell lost everything as a result. Except Kitty.

Churching: Up to the late 1960s, women who had given birth were expected to attend the ceremony of 'churching', which involved them being blessed and 'made pure again' (service unavailable to mothers of illegitimate kids). It was, presumably, the act of conceiving the child that caused the woman to be impure in the first place, which, by extension, makes all of human existence a sin!

Claddagh Ring: Perhaps because it's the handiest gadget ever invented to save girls the hassle of warding off unwanted attentions or encouraging wanted ones, the Claddagh Ring has attained global popularity. The ring features two hands holding a crowned heart, with the motto 'let love and friendship reign'. Association with Claddagh? No one has a clue. To practical matters. If you're a guy and want to

RIGHT HAND

SINGLE
(I'M LOOKING FOR LOVE)

RIGHT HAND

HAVE BOYFRIEND
(I'M FALLING IN LOVE)

LEFT HAND

MARRIED
(I WISH I'D NEVER BOUGHT THAT DAMN RING IN THE FIRST PLACE)

check the availability of the talent/avoid a kick in the goolies, note the following: worn on the right hand, heart facing out, she's up for courtin'; right hand, heart facing in, there's a burly boyfriend about to clatter you for staring at his mot's hand; left hand, crown out, forget it — she's hitched.

Clingfilm: Necessity is the mother of invention, and incredible as it may seem to anyone under thirty, stories abound of the lengths some would go to in order to get around the State's ban on condoms up to 1985. The manufacturers advised us to 'stretch the clingfilm tightly over the object, adhering it tightly to the sides and thus preventing any spillages.' And that's exactly what a lot of people did …

IT'S SO USEFUL! COVERING CASSEROLES, KEEPING BREAD FRESH, HAVING A QUICK SHAG, WRAPPING PASTRIES...

Coitus Interruptus: This was also a no-no, because 'the spilling of the seed' interferes with 'the natural consequences of sexual intercourse'. However, this being Ireland, priests

pulled out from denouncing it from the pulpit, as the details were too messy to go into. And, of course, their relative silence on the subject was taken as tacit approval. During this period, sales of tissue paper went through the roof.

Committee on Evil Literature:

Not, as the name suggests, a group of righteous individuals doing battle with the forces of darkness, but the group which preceded the Censorship Board. Sitting for only one year, 1926, their recommendations set the standards for the strict censorship of the decades ahead. Mentioned here only for their laughably dramatic title. For 'Evil' read 'Dirty'.

Condoms: These 'Sheaths of Satan' as the religious right called them, were banned from 1935 to 1979, when Charlie Haughey came up with his famous 'Irish solution to an Irish problem'. Under that legislation, a doctor could prescribe condoms to over 18s, which was, ironically, two years older than the legal age for marriage! What's more, the condoms had to be for 'bona fide' family planning purposes, (i.e. couples couldn't get them if they just wanted a quick shag). The law was, of course, unenforceable, as the government couldn't insist on surveillance of love-making couples to keep an eye on their bona fides. It wasn't until 1985 that condoms became available without prescription.

I'M NOT REALLY SURE MUGSY. I THINK WE BETTER STICK TO THE NYLON STOCKINGS.

1985

SWAG

Confession: The back door through which we could escape our guilt, especially over sex. As we fell helplessly into the jaws of passion,

aware of the inevitability of mortal sin, we comforted ourselves with the thought that tomorrow we would go to confession, say three Our Fathers and three Hail Marys and, Bob's yer uncle, we'd be grand with the Almighty again. So it seems God gave us guilt because he gave us sex, and confession because he gave us guilt. And in the divine plan, all three cancel each other out.

Contraceptive Ban: It's amazing to think that up to 1935, contraceptives were actually available in Ireland. Then the government decided to outlaw their sale or import, a ban that would last until 1979. Not content with banjaxing the country's economy for decades, people were now reminded of their incompetence at literally every conceivable moment.

Contraceptive Train: On 22 May 1971, a group from the Irish Women's Liberation Movement put the campaign for access to contraception back on track. They took a train over the border into the heathen UK and bought a gansey-load of contraceptives. Back in Dublin, they expected to be arrested for illegally importing the tools of the Devil, but the authorities went limp under the media spotlight, and the women were allowed pass. Thanks to the women on the 'Durex Express', a major border had just been crossed.

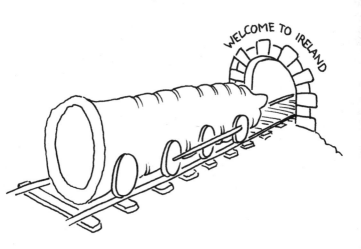

Courtship Rituals: In olden days these involved such passion-killers as being chaperoned for weeks before being allowed out of parental sight and then making sure that there was 'always room for the Holy Ghost' between you. Modern Irish courting rituals also severely restrict sexual activity, as they involve getting completely langered, jumping into bed, and then, before any funny business can happen, falling into an alcohol-induced coma.

Croke Park: Believe it or not, the hallowed turf of Croker had its own small part to play in Irish sex/love lore, thanks to a story that hit the headlines in Sept 2002. Why? This was the first time someone scored at Croke Park while there was no game taking place. A courting couple, showing passion normally reserved for All Ireland Finals, scaled the gates after mid-night, and by all accounts a lot of midfield action followed. It's not known how many shots they had, but they definitely had their own strip. The final result was that both midfielders were tackled by the Gardaí and sent off to court for a €500 fine. It will undoubtedly go down in GAA annals as a match that had a lot of physical contact.

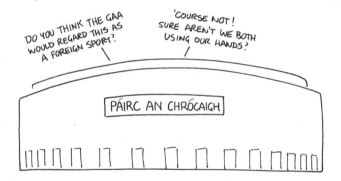

Dance Halls: 'Dens of Lust', 'Agencies of Satan', 'Vestibules of Hell' – dance halls as described by churchmen in the 1930s. In 1935 they persuaded the government to introduce the Public Dance Halls Act, which used the excuses of illicit drinking, safety concerns, etc to close down hundreds of dance halls. In reality, the intention of the Act was to rid Ireland of an 'immoral' influence and keep women firmly in their place – the kitchen.

Diarmuid & Gráinne: Ireland's greatest mythological lovers. Gráinne, the High King's daughter, was to wed the aged Fionn McCool, but at the wedding feast she cast a spell on Fionn's pal, Diarmuid, who she fancied rotten. Diarmuid fled with her and they spent sixteen years legging it around Ireland. Eventually, after a tussle with a magical boar,

Diarmuid lies dying and only water carried by Fionn will save him, but Fionn lets the water slip through his fingers and Diarmuid croaks. Incidentally, you'll find 'Diarmuid & Gráinne's beds' in forests or on mountains all over Ireland, reputedly spots where they slept. Evidence that Irish hotel prices were a rip-off even then.

Divorce: In early Celtic Ireland, grounds for divorce included sexual impotence due to gross obesity, telling tales about your love life or being a thief. Then, in 1937, divorce was banned under the Constitution, so you couldn't legally

dissolve your marriage on any grounds, including wife-beating, unfaithfulness, enduring
decades of mental torture, etc. It's ironic that
we can't say that the 1937 ban put us back in
the Dark Ages, as in many ways the Dark Ages
were much more enlightened.

Divorce Referenda: In 1986, Ireland
had its first divorce referendum. Six weeks
before the poll, a huge majority wanted to
remove the 1937 ban. Then the Catholic right
mobilised! Divorce would lead to the end of
the world, a plague of locusts, and so on ... The
ban was upheld. We got another shot at it in
1995 and it was almost a re-run – a big lead for

the 'Yes' campaign almost reversed by sensationalist fear tactics. The ban was lifted, but only by a tiny majority. Jaysus, what were we like?

Dungarvan (Its 15 minutes of fame):

In 1995, Dungarvan (Pop. 5,700), was briefly the focus of international media attention when Father Michael Kennedy declared from the pulpit that a local woman had deliberately slept with over sixty locals to infect them with AIDS. Cue hundreds of suspicious glances from wives at husbands who were suddenly fascinated by

the hymn sheet. The story spread like, well, a virus. Health experts, however, announced that the chances of a woman infecting so many men in this way were slim. Perversely, observers believe that this may have led to an increase in casual sex, which one assumes wasn't quite Fr Kennedy's intention.

Fallen Women: Not girls who turned up in A & E ward with cuts on their knees, but those who committed the greatest of all sins – getting preggers. The problem is that it's so bleedin' visible. A pregnant single girl wandering around the village for nine months, reminding everyone that they had wobbly bits, was

unthinkable. The solution was for their family to pack them off to a home so everyone could stop thinking about their thingies and return to singing songs about the Famine.

Fallen Men: As yet, historians have not found any records of this species, so it is assumed that all the fallen women were impregnated by some form of mysterious air-borne sperm.

Father Michael Cleary: In the mid-90s it emerged that another well-known cleric, Michael Cleary, had fathered a child. Known as 'the singing priest' Fr Cleary was out of tune with his own preaching on the evils of extra-

...AND THIS WEEK, INSTEAD OF A SERMON I'm GOING TO SING "IF I SAID YOU HAD A BEAUTIFUL BODY WOULD YOU HOLD IT AGAINST ME..."

marital sex and on priestly celibacy. It didn't really bother most people that he'd had a child, just that he'd had the nerve to make such a song and dance about his flock's sexual activities!

Football Team (giving birth to):

Nowadays, family size in Ireland conforms pretty much to the norm, i.e. 2.7465 kids. But at one

RELAX GUYS. THIS IS IRELAND. WE'LL PROBABLY ALL MAKE IT OUT OF HERE!

point, the average number of kids in an Irish family was 10! There are many explanations for these ultra-large families – no contraception, preference for male children, marriage age very low. The real reason is that Irish men and women are clearly the most fertile and sexually adept people on the planet.

Gay Ireland: Up to the 1970s, the only 'Gay' living in Ireland presented 'The Late Late Show'. For most Irish people, through ignorance, innocence or denial, homosexuality did not exist. But the wider world was opening up to us in the form of travel, films, multi-channel TV, literature, etc. And before we knew it, everyone had come out of the closet, in terms

of awareness at least, of the gay community's existence. Homosexual acts were decriminalised in 1993, and as a measure of how far we've come since then, we've had a couple of gay lads snogging on our most popular early evening soap. Ireland's first gay/lesbian Taoiseach can't be far behind.

Girlie Magazines: Up to 1996, the long-suffering men of Ireland had to go to great lengths to enjoy the beauties cavorting naked in *Playboy* magazine, as girlie mags were banned. To keep abreast of the latest centrefolds, you had to smuggle one in from some exotic place (like Newry or Birmingham) and risk being stigmatised for years. Nowadays you can get loads of mags with naked ladies. Or, for Mná na hÉireann, naked men. Did ye ever think we'd see the day?

Handfasting: Part of the ancient marriage ritual in which the couple getting married were literally hitched to each other with a rope around the wrists. In those enlightened days the trial marriage lasted 366 days. Then, if the wife

EH BRIDGET. ARE YOU SURE THIS WAS WHAT WAS MEANT BY HANDFASTING?

discovered that the hubby was, say, an alco with a sheep fetish, or he learned that his missus only changed her knickers once a year, they could tell each other to shag off when the period was up. This is where the term 'Tying the knot' originated. In some versions of the ritual, the knots couldn't be untied until the marriage had been consummated. Kinky, those Celts, eh?

In Dublin Magazine: From its launch in the 1970s, Dubliners knew that the easiest place to find sex was between the pages of this event guide. Not that it featured overt porn, but almost as titillating were the ads for Massage Parlours (brothels), the Small Ads for dirty videos and of course, its Personal Ads, some genuine, some not so. A typical one might run: 'Girl, 20s, large assets, seeks man for social intercourse. Bring money.' Who knows, maybe she really did just want to have a chat and the money was to feed the gas meter?

Internet: A brief search using the words 'Ireland' and 'sex' reveals that inhibition has become a dirty word. Any sexual liaison can be arranged – man/woman, man/man, woman/woman, couple/woman; you name it. Want sex toys, edible lingerie or a vibrating bed with mirrored ceiling? No problem. And apparently a big hit with Irish couples are silk bands for tying up one's partner. Must be something to do with our 700 years of bondage.

Irish Family Planning Association:

Without the IFPA's tireless fight for contraceptive rights, it's probably safe to say that our largely impotent political masters would still be wondering if a spermicidal jelly would be nice with custard.

Kissing: Mothers and priests didn't discourage the widespread belief among young Irish girls that you could get pregnant through French kissing. Possibly where the word 'misconception' came from.

Knock Marriage Bureau: Set up in 1969 and run by a local priest, the bureau has been responsible for arranging almost 900 marriages. And, at just €80 a pop, you could end up with a marriage licence for less than a TV licence.

I FELL IN LOVE THROUGH THE KNOCK MARRIAGE BUREAU

NOW THAT'S WHAT I CALL A MIRACLE

Lad Lane: The most appropriately named lane in Ireland, if not in the world. Lad, in case you're unaware, is a Dublin slang word for, eh, willy. And Lad Lane is the place where you're most likely to see one in action, as it is frequented by ladies of the night. It's probably just a coincidence, but it's nice to think that Dublin's 'working girls' chose Lad Lane as a place of business because they've got a really good sense of humour.

Lap Dancing Clubs: First appeared in Dublin in the mid-1990s and have since spread to every corner of the country. Most of the performers are English girls or from Eastern Europe; Irish girls are still probably worried they'll end up dancing for their Da. In 2002, the

shocked residents of the Kildare village of Milltown discovered that they had a lap dancing club in their tiny backwater. Surely not what De Valera envisioned – comely maidens lap-dancing at the crossroads?

Late Late Show, The: The Catholic, right-wing politician Oliver J Flanagan once remarked that there was no sex in Ireland before TV. More accurately, there was no sex before 'The Late Late Show'. Its host, Gay Byrne, shocked us unworldly Paddies by shooting the breeze with lesbian nuns or demonstrating the use of a condom with his finger. In an earlier show, Gay had a mock version of the 'Mr & Mrs'

quiz in which he asked a contestant what she wore in bed on her honeymoon night. Her joking reply of 'nothing' brought a torrent of condemnation. How innocent we were ...

Lent: In the old days, you were encouraged to abstain from many things during Lent: Meat, drinking, sweets, dancing, getting married, carnal pleasures, swearing, general merrymaking. That left knitting.

Lisdoonvarna Matchmaking Festival: Lisdoonvarna in County Clare
was originally famed for the healing power of its natural spa. Nowadays, Lisdoonvarna invites

Marriage: In Brehon times there were up to ten forms of marriage. In 20th century Ireland, marriage had only one form – insoluble. So you had better not make a pig's arse of picking your mate, because whatever happened you'd be stuck with him/her for eternity. The other thing about Irish marriage was that it was the only way legitimately to get laid. This was called the 15,000-night stand.

I NEVER THOUGHT WHEN WE GOT MARRIED WE'D END UP HATING EACH OTHERS GUTS SO MUCH.

ME NEITHER. ESPECIALLY SINCE THAT WAS ONLY 2 WEEKS AGO.

Massage Parlours: In the 1980s/1990s anyone in search of a genuine massage was likely to find parts of his anatomy tended to that wouldn't be found in the Physiotherapist's

Handbook. Ads featuring 'Massage Parlour' usually meant 'Brothel'. But common as this knowledge was, numerous Garda raids indicated that countless politicians, clergy and lawyers made this mistake and went seeking treatment for a particular muscle which had gone into spasm.

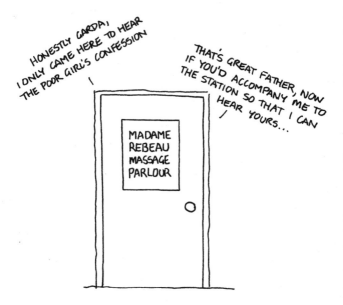

Masturbation: Bodily self-abuse, self-defilement or self-pollution, as it used to be called, besides being a mortal sin, produced a range of side-effects that were God's way of punishing us. Among these were blindness, stunted growth, gradual insanity, growth of hair on palms, acne. At least that's what our short, spotty, hairy, specky lune of a teacher told us.

Monto: 'The Monto' was Dublin's thriving red light district from 1870 until 1925. At one time, up to 1,200 ladies offered their wares in the Montgomery Street (now Foley Street) area, making it Europe's largest red light district. The Monto was frequented by many notables, including King Edward VII, presumably so he could personally acquaint his subjects with the royal sceptre.

Most Lustful Man in Ireland: The title perhaps goes to the last High King of Ireland, Ruaidhrí Ó Conchobhair, (died in 1198, probably from exhaustion). Old Ruaidrhí is reputed to have had his wicked way with so many women that it became too much for the Pope, who had to satisfy himself with a handful.

He offered to forgive Ruaidhrí if he would con-
fine himself to having sex with just six women.
Ruaidhrí's reply? 'You mean, at the same time?'

Movie Bans: There have been thousands
over the last century, including *Brief Encounter*
(1946) for an extra-marital affair, *Ulysses*, (1967)
for obscene language, *The Life of Brian*, (1979)
for blasphemy, From *Dusk 'till Dawn* (1996) for
violence. But for every three banned, ten 'dirty'
movies were allowed through – after they'd
been slashed to ribbons. See, with movies, it's
easy to snip out people's naughty bits. This
resulted in scenes like:

Jane: 'Frank! I want you to make me feel like a wom—'

Frank: 'I better get to work, it's almost nine.'

Jane: 'You sure you won't join me in the shower?'

Frank: 'Yes, waiter, I'll have the steak.'

Pill, The: Incredibly, given the era's anti-contraception frenzy, the Pill was available here in 1963. Had they suddenly decided to allow us let our hair down, not to mention our undies? 'Course not! Doctors could prescribe the Pill only as a cycle regulator. And good Catholic women using it thus would never stoop to taking advantage of its other side-effect: consequence-free sex. Unfortunately, if your doctor wouldn't prescribe the Pill, the only other legal oral contraceptive available was the word 'No.'

SHE SAYS SHE'S TAKING THE THE PILL AS A CYCLE REGULATOR.

YEAH SURE. AND I SUPPOSE THAT'S WHY THEY CALL HER 'THE BICYCLE!'

Polygamy: In pre-Christian Ireland, it was accepted practice for men (particularly wealthy ones) to have several wives, and though the Church opposed this when they arrived, polygamy endured for centuries. The official reason for having lots of wives was to have lots of male heirs. The unofficial reason was so that rich men could have an unlimited supply of sex.

The result was that these guys often had over thirty kids! Imagine what it was like trying to get a turn in the bathroom in the morning?

Pregnancy: When occurring out of wedlock, it was traditional to describe the pregnant lass by one of the following quaint old Irish phrases: 'Up the pole', 'Up the flue', 'In the family way', 'A bun in the oven', 'About to drop a chisler'. For the correct usage of these expressions, please note that they were traditionally muttered under the breath.

Queen Maeve: A definite contender for Ireland's most lustful woman, Maeve supposedly lived around the first century B.C. and her most famous adventure is recorded in The Táin (The Cattle Raid of Cooley). But it was her sexual adventures that were really legendary. As a sort of staff incentive scheme, Maeve would offer her 'willing thighs' to her bravest warriors and was reputed to have had as many as thirty men a day! To think this sex-machine's face used to grace our £1 note ...

Rhythm Method: The only form of family planning officially endorsed by Church and State up to almost the end of the last century. But because they were too embarrassed to fully explain the technique to anyone, based as it was on the woman's menstrual cycle, lots of girls decided to interpret the title as meaning it was safe to have sex immediately after a bit of fervent dancing to the local showband.

School Dances: For many an Irish youth, this was the first contact he/she would have with the opposite sex. Actually, contact is too strong a word, as any boob/chest interaction would earn you a poke of a stick in the ear from the supervising Brother/nun. Nuns reputedly wouldn't let girls wear shiny shoes in

case boys could see a reflection of their knickers. Only dancing and talking was allowed. The talking inevitably got around to getting the hell out of there and finding somewhere to have a grope.

Sex: In Ireland this was an eight-letter word spelled m-a-r-r-i-a-g-e. Pre-marital sex was not so much frowned upon as trodden upon. But there was a possible escape clause. If you were chastised for considering pre-marital sex, you could always inform the priest that it wasn't pre-marital if you never intended to get married.

Sex Education: In Ireland, education was traditionally provided by religious orders for whom sex did not officially exist – so no need for sex education. Parents stuck to 'the stork brought you' story, so sex education was confined to sniggered whispers behind the school shed. Here you had your first lesson in the biology of the opposite sex's body, the geometry of which bit went where and the mathematical impossibility of this ever happening to you. It was also where every thirteen-year-old first learned that intercourse wasn't the exam you sat in 3rd year.

Sheela-na-Gigs: Ancient stone carvings of women blatantly displaying their naughty bits. The carvings predate Christianity and were possibly part of early fertility rites and a celebration of female sexuality. The gas thing is that the place you're most likely to find one of these shameless hussies is above the doorway of a church!

MAYBE IT'S LIKE SOME ANCIENT FORM OF PLAYBOY MAGAZINE...

Spike, The: Not the yoke in O'Connell Street, but a short-lived RTE TV series in the late 1970s that was as hotly debated as the Keane/McCarthy affair. Episode 5 featured a woman posing nude for an art class. Of course, the entire country tuned in to watch. Condemnation (and axing of the series) swiftly followed, and, most famously, the founder of the

League of Decency suffered a heart attack after watching the scene. Imagine how they'd have reacted to 'Sex and the City'?

St Valentine: The patron saint of mushy greeting cards ... sorry ... love, whose remains are reputed to lie in Dublin's Whitefriar Street church, a gift from Pope Gregory XVI in 1835. Before he was martyred in Rome on 14 February, AD269, he miraculously cured his jailor's blind daughter and sent her a message signed 'from your Valentine'. But that's probably a load of crap. He's now a global industry, his name adorning cards, inflatable hearts, even sex toys! .The inscription on his casket reads: Roses are red, violets are blue … (Only kidding).

Terms of Endearment: Expressions of endearment *as Gailge* can be found in Irish literature stretching back millennia. Among the most popular to survive are: *A ghrá mo chroí* (Love of my heart), *Mo mhúirnín bán* (My beautiful darling), and *Póg mo thóin* (Kiss my arse). This last has the benefit that it can be used both as an expression of anger and of affection.

Unfortunate Girls: The term given to prostitutes in the early part of the last century. In those days many girls arrived in the capital from impoverished rural homes in search of work, often to be abused by their employers, and then turning to prostitution in desperation. Today, of course, that's all changed. Now the girls come from impoverished countries in Eastern Europe to be abused by their employers.

Viagra: Given Ireland's sexual history, it's paradoxical that the small town of Ringaskiddy in Cork should be the place that, since the mid

1990s, has been giving a lift to people's sex lives all over the world. Since US drug giant Pfizer erected their Viagra plant, the area's previously limp economy has grown enormously and earned it the nickname Viagra Falls. The local name for the drug is 'De Pfizer Riser' and rumours have abounded of a baby boom in the area due to emissions from the plant, but the hard facts refute this. Aside from that, it seems that unless sex suddenly becomes unpopular, the town's fortunes will continue to rise and rise.

Virginity: One of the traditional Irish ways to scare girls into retaining their virginity was for a nun to pull the petals off a flower, then ask one of the class to come up and replace them. Impossible, of course, and it was equally impossible to get your virginity back. And what man would want a flower with no petals? This practice gave the English language the term 'to deflower'. It also gave us a huge number of really pissed-off gardeners.

E BOOK OF FECKIN' IRISH SLANG THAT'S
HE BOOK OF DEADLY IRISH QUOTATIONS
LATHERIN' ON ABOUT THE BOOK OF IRISH
E WAS JARRED AT A HOOLEY THE FECKIN
OR DACENT PEOPLE'S EYES THE BOOK OF
HEN YOU WERE A LITTLE GURRIER THE
OU GO ON THE BATTER WITH A SHOWER OI
HAT'S GREAT CRAIC FOR CUTE HOORS
UOTATIONS SOME SMART FECKER IN THI
OOK OF IRISH SONGS YER OUL' FELLA
OOLEY THE FECKIN' BOOK OF IRISH SEX &
YES THE BOOK OF LUVELY IRISH RECIPI
TTLE GURRIER THE FECKIN' BOOK OF
ATTER WITH A SHOWER OF SAVAGES THE
RAIC FOR CUTE HOORS AND BOWSIES TH
MART FECKER IN THE PUB IS ALWAYS BLA
ER OUL' FELLA ALWAYS SANG WHEN HE V
F IRISH SEX & LOVE THAT'S NOT FIT FOR
ISH RECIPES YER MA USETA MAKE WHE
OOK OF IRISH SAYINGS FOR WHEN YOU
GES THE BOOK OF FECKIN' IRISH SLANG
OWSIES THE BOOK OF DEADLY IRISH QUO
LWAYS BLATHERIN' ON ABOUT THE BOO
ANG WHEN HE WAS JARRED AT A HOOL